T0157590

TRYING TO DO HIS PART

The Life Story of

Retired Major Cecil Eldridge Johnston

By Virginia Bradshaw

iUniverse, Inc.
New York   Bloomington

Trying To Do His Part
The Life Story of Retired Major Cecil Eldridge Johnston

Copyright © 2010, 2012 by Virginia Bradshaw

All rights reserved. No part of this book may be used or reproduced by any means, graphic, electronic, or mechanical, including photocopying, recording, taping or by any information storage retrieval system without the written permission of the publisher except in the case of brief quotations embodied in critical articles and reviews.

iUniverse books may be ordered through booksellers or by contacting:

iUniverse
1663 Liberty Drive
Bloomington, IN 47403
www.iuniverse.com
1-800-Authors (1-800-288-4677)

Because of the dynamic nature of the Internet, any Web addresses or links contained in this book may have changed since publication and may no longer be valid. The views expressed in this work are solely those of the author and do not necessarily reflect the views of the publisher, and the publisher hereby disclaims any responsibility for them.

ISBN: 978-1-4502-6315-3 (sc)
ISBN: 978-1-4502-6316-0 (ebook)

Printed in the United States of America

iUniverse rev. date: 6/8/2012

COVER PHOTO CAPTION: Two American soldiers on patrol through the watery streets of a bombed-out village as they seek out hidden German snipers, on the Italian front in the Appennine Mountains 01 April 1945. (Photo by Margaret Bourke-White//Time Life Pictures/Getty Images)

CONTENTS

I dedicate this to two good wives and
five good children.
- Retired Maj. Cecil E. Johnston

CHAPTER ONE

Born in Those Oklahoma Hills

Retired U.S. Army Maj. Cecil Eldridge Johnston was born on a hot July 27th, 1920, to William Arthur Johnston, a 24-year-old sharecropper, and his 20-year-old one-fourth Cherokee Indian wife, Idaho Montana Smith Johnston.

His first home was a two-room house on a hillside near the tree-shaded North Boggy River in Atoka County- almost Coal County- in southeastern Oklahoma. The house consisted of one family bedroom and a multi-purpose kitchen. It wasn't fancy but by 1920s standards, it wasn't bad, Johnston remembers.

The river in places was 20 to 30 feet across, in others, 10 to 20 feet, still a lot of water. During spring rains, it would often go out of its banks. People had to know the safe spots to build houses to avoid being flooded every year.

At flood stage, the river's currents were so strong they could move almost anything, even concrete bridge supports.

Post oaks, blackjack oaks, pecan trees and pines flourished in the area. It was home to numerous deer that liked to get in gardens and eat the vegetables; raccoons and opossums.

William Arthur Johnston worked hard at growing corn, oats and some cotton, which Cecil Johnston helped pick as a boy.

Idaho Montana Johnston kept house, cooked big meals and raised nine children. Conserving their water that had to be hauled in and washing clothes in the creek was part of her way of life.

Her father, John Smith, owned the farm, had cleared the land for it, and built not only his own home but the house for the William Arthur and Idaho Montana Johnston family. The farm was right where Lake Atoka is today.

John Smith was Cecil Johnston's beloved "Grandpa." To a lot of other folks, he was called "Whiskey John."

As a child Johnston didn't know why his mama wouldn't let him go down to his grandfather's house if she didn't go with him.

"I thought my Grandpa walked on water and didn't get his feet wet," Johnston said.

Grandpa Smith had a nice home and was a smart man, Johnston recalls. "Grandpa knew more about farming than anyone he knew. He knew about rotating crops. He was really, really sharp and way ahead of his time."

He had ducks and chickens and geese. "The geese would chase me under the porch and he would come rescue me."

He planted a big garden and told young Cecil Johnston it was his job to look after it, although half-Cherokee Grandma Smith and Johnston's mama also worked in it. "He was nice to me."

Smith always had fruit trees, too. "Grandpa showed me how to put the fruit up on the roof to dry." He dried apricots and peaches. If a rain was coming, he'd take them down and store them in the barn until the showers passed. He always had fruit for wintertime meals.

He had five children who all lived nearby and he helped them all.

Smith built a school for all the children in the area and helped hire the teacher. It was a one-room school and the one in which Cecil Johnston began his education.

The teacher had one class in one size and another on the other side of the room for kids who were a different size. The class a student attended was decided "by how big you were," Johnston said.

Smith was a county commissioner when Johnston was a little boy.

He built roads and houses everywhere he lived. People in that part of the country who wanted to work, Smith put them to work.

There was a man who had 20 kids, Johnston remembers. Smith taught him how to cut cross ties for the railroads. He wanted one-fourth, when Smith was offering him one-third of the proceeds from selling the railroad ties.

"The man thought one-fourth was more than one-third. Grandpa got down on the ground and drew two pies and showed him one-third was more."

The employee said, "Mr. John, you're an honest man."

Smith grew corn on his farm. The only way to move it to market was by wagon or horseback.

One day they were gathering corn. Johnston and his Aunt Marie were in the seat of a wagon and people were throwing corn into the back

All of a sudden, the horses started running round and round and the wagon went flying. Smith, Johnston's dad and his Uncle R.A. stopped them. No one was hurt.

"Grandpa said, 'what happened?' Aunt Marie said the horse's bonnet came off, meaning he got his blinders off.

"Everybody was out helping. It was lucky Grandpa had a wooden fence so the horses would turn around and go in a circle," Johnston said.

While horse power was the only way to move corn on the cob to market, it was cheaper to sell it in liquid form in a bottle.

"His main way of making money was making moonshine" whiskey, Johnston said.

"The preacher where Grandma went to church said don't worry about where the money came from. He said just keep on bringing the money in. We'll bless it and go on and use it.

"I didn't know what revenooers and moonshiners were, but that's why Mama wouldn't let me go down there by myself."

Smith had a thriving business in those Prohibition days. He made it, sold it himself and Johnston's Aunt Ruby, one of his mother's sisters, sold it from her house in town.

Johnston can remember as a little boy, seeing a lot of cars around Aunt Ruby's house. "Mama wouldn't let me go over there because she didn't want me to be around whiskey," Johnston said.

"Grandpa was a business person. He put everybody to work that wanted to work. Aunt Ruby liked her job."

Smith paid law enforcement to not raid his operations but he went to prison for one of his sons.

The son's charge had something to do with Oklahoma's Prohibition laws and liquor revenue.

Smith pleaded guilty for his son's offense and was sent to El Reno (Oklahoma) federal prison. He was in prison less than a year when he became terminally ill. The authorities sent him home to die.

Grandpa Smith was a good farmer, a good businessman– and a good man. He just used his own unique way of getting his corn crop to market.

CHAPTER TWO

Little Florence Was Ablaze

It was Cecil Johnston's job as eldest child, to help look after his brothers and sisters. "Don't you let any of those kids get hurt," his mother would tell him.

He did his job so well he once saved his little sister Florence's life.

One day the boy was milking cows when Florence, nine years younger than him, locked the door to their house- and caught her dress on fire.

Cecil Johnston broke open the door, ran in, put out the flames and carried her to a doctor's home. "You saved her life," the physician told him.

Dr. Cullums rushed the child to the nearest hospital but in the next several days it appeared she was dying. A doctor, visiting from the Shrine Hospital in Massachusetts, took one look and said, "stop putting paraffin on her burns and removing it every day. You're killing her by degrees." He told the medical personnel what they should do instead, and the little girl survived.

Johnston said that years later, he joined the Shrine Club because "they saved my sister's life and I wanted to be a part of them."

In addition to Cecil Johnston, who was born in 1920, William Arthur Johnston and Idaho Montana Smith Johnston's large family included Bertha Juanita Johnston, born Nov. 24, 1921, and died of diphtheria Dec. 17, 1926, shortly after her fifth birthday;

Walter Edison Johnston, born Sept. 27, 1924; Chester Ira Johnston, born March 30, 1926; Florence Lorene Johnston Burns, born April 10, 1929; Willie Ione Johnston Austin, born Sept. 27, 1931, now deceased;

Karl Kenneth Johnston, born Nov. 9, 1938; John Wesley Johnston, born Oct. 29, 1940; and Leslie Paul Johnston, born Sept. 24, 1943, also now deceased.

William Arthur Johnston was 89 years old when he died in Cecil Johnston's arms in February 1986, in Shawnee, Oklahoma.

He died two months after his wife, Idaho Montana Johnston, passed away on Dec. 11, 1985, also in Shawnee. She was 85. Cecil Johnston was with her, too, at the time of her death.

The Johnston family has been traced back to early Scotland centuries before Christopher Columbus was born. A family history states that the first Johnston of note was Sir Gilbert de Johnston who lived in Lockerbie in the 1200s.

It has been established the family came from Annandale, Scotland. At least one of the first, if not the first Johnston to come to America was Dr. John Johnston, who was born in Edinburgh, Scotland in 1661, and immigrated to Perth Amboy, New Jersey, in 1685. He held many important positions including a four-year period as mayor of New York City.

The Johnston family was prominent in New Jersey and Virginia. General A.S. Johnston was born in Kentucky in 1803 and was one of the great Civil War generals.

A family history notes that the Johnstons were Democrats and Methodists, always honorable community leaders who were never convicted of an offense. (Cecil Johnston's grandfather who was a community leader but went to prison to protect his son, was a Smith.)

For Cecil Johnston, life was not easy growing up in a large family on a farm in the '20s, only 15 or 20 years after Oklahoma became a state in 1907, and especially during the Great Depression.

One of his earliest memories was of how the kids "always had to wait for the second helpings; we never did get to eat at the head table.

"I grew up on biscuits and gravy. When it was water gravy, times were hard. Sometimes in the Depression, it was water gravy."

But part of the fun, he said, was doing something to help.

He helped with the family's garden; the chickens they raised for eggs and food; the cow they kept for milk and the annual project of fattening a pig that was butchered in the fall and its meat hung in the smokehouse for winter meals.

"One time when I was 5 or 6 or 7, I was helping make sorghum and my brother Walter was watching. He was about 2, and just learning to walk good.

"After two or three days, you have a pretty good pile of ashes. Under the ashes were coals that were still red hot.

"Walter ran on top of it. Our dad pulled him out of it, but his feet were burned so bad they put him in the hospital.

"His toes grew back together and they had to cut them loose."

Walter had to learn to walk again, Johnston said. Luckily, "he was young enough that he overcame all those things."

They raised sugar cane for the sorghum and when it was sorghum making time, everybody who was working on it, got some of it, he said.

Johnston also remembers once when a panther came through their place. "His cry was like a woman crying. Mama pulled the curtains. She told me not to look out the window.

"I heard the horses get out of the barn and run out into the field. But Mama wouldn't let us look out because the panther might break into the house," Johnston said.

"As a kid growing up on North Boggy Creek," Johnston saw many things. One memory is still etched in his mind, perhaps three-quarters of a century later.

"I once saw a black man shot to death and he wasn't doing anything wrong that I knew about. He was on public property, the roadway. His son was with him and was about the same age as me."

Johnston and the son became "real good friends. I made a special point to go and see him when I came back from the Army. I found him working as a janitor at the state capitol in Oklahoma City.

"We renewed our friendship.

"This reminds me of my mama telling me that you should not mistreat anybody because of the color of their skin."

There was also some prejudice against Indians in that period, too, Johnston indicated, but not to that extent.

In summer, the Johnston family slept on the porch to escape the heat inside. On especially hot nights, his mother would advise them to sprinkle a little water on their beds "and it will stay cool until you go to sleep."

"We made our own fun," Johnston said. "You learned to swing off a grapevine across the creek- not when the creek was up, of course. You did a lot of things that were work but were fun.

"Mama would have me build little fires to keep the mosquitoes away. I made them where it was all gravel, poured a little water on the coals and it would start smoking and that would run the mosquitoes away."

Johnston started his education in the one-room school outside of Stringtown, Oklahoma, that his grandfather had built and staffed with its one teacher. Johnston spent his first two years at that school.

He later attended school in Atoka, Coalgate, Earlsboro, Pauls Valley and Bethany, all in eastern or central Oklahoma, and Electra, Texas. He went to school in Earlsboro at three different time periods, graduating from Earlsboro High School in 1939.

Johnston attended Draughn's Business College in Oklahoma City after high school but didn't graduate because he couldn't go to school and work two full-time jobs at the same time. He was trying to help his family survive because it was still the Depression.

Johnston much later received a bachelor's degree from the University of Maryland.

CHAPTER THREE

"All I Knew Was to Work, but I Made It Fun"

The Johnston family left their home on Grandpa Smith's farm when Cecil Johnston was about 8 years old.

They moved to Butler's Place, a farm in Atoka County, between Atoka and Coalgate. William Arthur Johnston was a sharecropper, which meant he farmed land owned by someone else and shared proceeds from the harvest with the landowner.

They stayed there a short time, before moving on to Earlsboro about 1928 or 1929.

Earlsboro, about nine miles east of Shawnee in Pottawatomie County was at the height of a multi-million dollar oil boom.

Oil was discovered when the No. 1 Joe Ingram well came in at Earlsboro March 1, 1926, and began producing 200 barrels a day. That summer, the No. 1 Simpson blew in at Saint Louis, a small community in southeast Pottawatomie County.

At the peak of production, Pottawatomie County oil wells were delivering more than 120,000 barrels a day. More than $1 billion worth of oil was pumped from the Earlsboro and Greater Seminole pools between 1926 and '29.

"One of the things I remember as a kid," Johnston said, "was oil shooting through the derricks and seeing 2x12 boards flying like toothpicks."

Earlsboro had gone from a sleepy little community to a booming city of 20,000 almost over night.

"A man named Olin Sangster who was from a foreign country, built his house on the side of a hill and had chickens. There were so many new people in Earlsboro, he pushed the chickens out, put a floor in the chicken house and moved it close to the creek.

"We lived in that. I don't think we stayed there a long time. My dad was working in the oil fields."

Earlsboro's streets, "I mean, were muddy," Johnston recalls. The heavy oil field equipment moving through the town daily made ruts "so deep you could hardly walk across them, especially when it was muddy."

However, by 1928, not every street in the boom town was like that, just nearly every one. In that year, two to four blocks of Earlsboro Main Street were paved with concrete, making it one of the earliest state towns to have some concrete paving.

Johnston was probably in third grade. The family stayed in Earlsboro 18 months to two years. William Arthur Johnston worked as an oiler, one who oiled the equipment on the rigs.

"When they were pumping, all that stuff had to have oil or it would stick." One day, "the boss got on my daddy. My daddy threw the oil can down and left," Johnston said.

He moved his family to Bethany and got a job with an oil company there. "Later on, he became a butcher and did that for most of the rest of his life."

From Bethany, the family moved to Pauls Valley where the elder Johnston finally found work- which turned out to be his first job as a butcher.

It was the Depression by then and William Arthur Johnston had looked all over for work. Cecil Johnston knew that because his mother told him the only money they had coming in was from the newspaper route he started carrying when he was about 12 years old.

Cecil Johnston began delivering the Daily Oklahoman in Pauls Valley and continued at Atoka and Earlsboro. That was just one of his jobs as a teenager, however.

"All I knew was to work but I tried to make fun out of everything I did," he said.

When Cecil Johnston was in about the sixth grade, William Arthur Johnston- still following the oil fields- moved his family to Electra, Texas, west of Wichita Falls, Texas, and south of Frederick, Oklahoma.

Until then, Cecil Johnston had been known by his middle and last names, Eldridge Johnston. But the teacher at Electra didn't understand that.

"She slammed her ruler on my desk and said, 'what's your name, kid? Don't you have another name?'

"I said, yes ma'm. She asked what it was. I said, Cecil. She said, 'from now on your name is Cecil.'

"About a month later, my mother came to the classroom door and said she had come to get Eldridge. The teacher said, 'I don't have anyone named Eldridge.'

"Mama said, yes you do. That's him sitting right over there.' "

Perhaps before that school year was over, the family moved back to Earlsboro where his dad resumed working as a butcher and Cecil Johnston again delivered the Oklahoman.

He was in seventh and eighth grades in that period. He remembers Bruce Jenkins was his teacher.

He also remembers getting bitten by "a Heinz 57" dog on his paper route and having to take the required 21 shots against rabies.

He received the vaccinations in his arm or stomach. "They were real, real painful."

Earlsboro still had pumping oil wells at that time.

Johnston learned to play "a very select number of songs in the Methodist hymnal" on the piano at church "because my teacher was nice to me and let me learn as much as I could," he said. In return, he played the piano for Sunday school and youth Bible study on Sunday nights. "I thought I was walking in tall cotton."

One of Cecil Johnston's chores was to drive the family's cow from their lot every morning to a field where there was a pond. When he came home from school he would bring her back to their place so he could milk her.

They moved on to Coalgate where his father worked a year or so as a butcher before returning to Earlsboro.

Cecil Johnston was in tenth grade when they went back to Earlsboro for the third time. He finished high school at Earlsboro.

Years later, when he turned in an application for a top secret classification during World War II, "the FBI sent it back and said 'you can't possibly have gone to that many schools.' I wrote back and said, 'you ask the schools.'

"I never heard any more and got the top secret clearance."

"Times were hard," Cecil Johnston said of those Depression-era days. Kenneth Faudree, a welder in Atoka who was Aunt Ruby's second husband, "would bring Mama money because he knew that Mama and us didn't have any money.

"Back in those days, welders normally had pretty good jobs. We were on a starvation diet. We had water gravy, so times were really really hard."

When he was in ninth grade at Coalgate, Cecil Johnston went to Mr. Hudson, one of two brothers who owned and operated Hudson's Big Country Store in Coalgate and Little Country Store in Atoka.

"Each ran one of the stores. In their Big Country Store, they had everything under the sun," Johnston said.

He worked at the store in Coalgate for a while "as a flunkie," then went to see the brother in Atoka, where his father was working at the Little Country Store.

"I told him, 'you used to have a produce area where you sold chickens.' Mr. Hudson said he 'let the guy go because he wasn't making me any money.'

"I said I'll do it for free for a week. If I make you money, you hire me and pay me what I'm worth.' Mr. Hudson said 'I can't lose on that.' "

Johnston bought their chickens, fed them chicken feed- and oyster shells, (which immediately made them gain weight) and was able to sell them for more than he paid for them. Hudson said 'you've made money. You did real good,' and hired him for the summer.

"That's where I learned to talk to people about whatever business I was trying to sell," Johnston said.

This was in addition to the teenager's paper route

CHAPTER FOUR

It Really WAS Pretty Boy Floyd

One of Cecil Johnston's varied experiences happened when he was a schoolboy delivering morning newspapers in Earlsboro during its oil boom days.

He received his papers downtown and folded them on the floor in the back of an all-night café.

"One time a man came in early, ate and visited with people in the café. Me, I just listened," Johnston said.

It seemed the man was called Pretty Boy Floyd.

"He came in early two or three times after I found out who he was, and just hung around. Later, I realized he was casing the bank across the street, to rob it at a later time," Johnston said.

He was also there when Floyd staged the armed robbery. The famous Oklahoma bank robber "dropped some of his shells and I picked them up," Johnston recalled.

Pretty Boy Floyd "robbed and gave it to the needy in town and around Earlsboro. My daddy worked in the oil fields with his brother.

"You can find out a lot of things by just listening," Johnston concludes.

The Johnston family moved back to Earlsboro from Coalgate when he was still in tenth grade.

Cecil Johnston got a job at a nice hotel in Earlsboro that probably was built in the town's oil rich days of the 1920s.

"It was janitorial work, anything, as long as I had a job."

Part of his pay was a pig. He took it home, "fed it milk and slop, and fattened it up."

In the fall, after frost, it was butchered. It provided meat all winter, Johnston said.

He held that part-time job during his junior and senior years at Earlsboro High School.

Johnston also made time during those two years, for playing forward on the Earlsboro High School basketball team. "Officially, we lost every game we played," he remembers. "We weren't as good as the people we were playing. And they were taller."

He also played baseball for Earlsboro. "We did pretty good. We were more on our turf. We won over half of those games," said Johnston, who played catcher.

When he graduated, he went to Oklahoma City and worked at several businesses.

Johnston worked in the meat department of a grocery store in Nichols Hills, Oklahoma City's most exclusive neighborhood, at two downtown drug stores simultaneously and delivered Pepsi Cola.

At the grocery store, "a lady would come in and say she wanted ground beef but not what was in their show window. I'd say, I'll get it in the back. It's just for people like you. I would sell it to people and tell them that when you cook it, it'll melt in your mouth.

"I was making money for the boss and he liked it."

Johnston worked at Veazey's and V.E. Cowdrey drug stores in Oklahoma City while trying to go to Draughn's Business College.

"I would go up there (to Oklahoma City) and stay with a friend," he said. He would work eight hours for Cowdrey, then go over to Veazey's because they stayed open until 10 p.m.

"I was trying to help my folks survive because we were still in the Depression."

One of his jobs was working the soda fountain and delivering prescription drugs on his bicycle.

One customer was a German man who wanted beer at room temperature. "They told me when he comes in, to give him a warm beer from the store room. He took it. I thought he was easier to satisfy than most of the people. All he wanted to do was drink his hot beer."

Later on, Johnston was a Pepsi Cola delivery man's helper. They delivered to "beer joints and stores in northeast Oklahoma City." But some of the patrons in the bars "were real drunk." He thought that might not be the safest of jobs.

While he didn't graduate from Draughn's because he couldn't go to school and work two jobs, Johnston said he got as much business education as he could.

"And I met a lot of nice people over the years."

Johnston joined the National Guard around September or October 1939, "and that took the rest of my time. They paid you by the number of hours you put in."

He was still in it when it was mobilized as the 45th Division in 1941.

Johnston remembers his first trip to Louisiana on maneuvers. "They gave me a pack I had to carry on my back. We walked and rode in 2 ½ ton trucks."

It was his first trip out of Oklahoma. "I looked in the pack. Somebody had put in pins to pitch a tent. I didn't know what they were. They all laughed at me."

He got sunburned.

Johnston was digging latrines when a lieutenant came over and told him to get out because he'd been doing all the work and the others were just sitting around.

"I had a real learning experience. I was a green recruit, didn't know nothin' but working on a farm and going to school."

He was 19 or 20 when he joined the National Guard. "I really enjoyed the 45th Division part of it. I got to be a supply sergeant and later on, got to be first sergeant.

"I started off at $21 a month, and got only $17 of the $21." His first paycheck was $15.

"I told Mama I'd send her $21, so I washed khakis for 50 cents or a dollar a payday. Before it was over, I had pretty near everybody in the company owing me money."

He kept a little book in the supply room listing who owed him and how much.

"Everybody paid me except a boy who went AWOL. I decided to just lose that $20 because that boy had more problems than that."

Johnston never did figure out why he just got $17, rather than the $21. But he was able to send his mother $21 a month as he had told her he would.

"I felt that was pretty good. I wasn't making this much at Earlsboro."

They were mobilized sometime in the first six months of 1941. "We were trying to get ready to go overseas or whatever they wanted us to do."

In the spring of '41, after being mobilized, they were sent to Fort Sill, Oklahoma. He remembers one of his first jobs there was dragging dirt in toe sacks for making foundations for tents.

Cecil Johnston's parents, Idaho Montana Smith Johnston
and William Arthur Johnston about 1920.

Johnston was Earlsboro High School basketball
team member No. 00 holding the ball that reads
"EHS-'38-'39," in the first row of players.

Johnston as a "private in the rear ranks," as he describes it, about the time his National Guard unit was mobilized in early 1941. He was probably in the Wichita Mountains near Fort Sill, Okla.

Johnston had worked his way up to sergeant in this picture taken early in his military career.

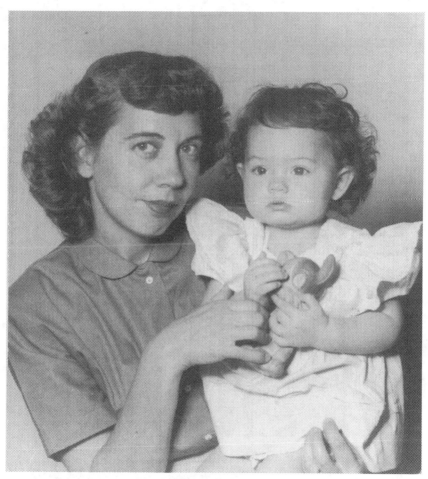

Johnston's first wife, the late Inez Johnston, with their
young daughter, Patricia, in the early 1950s

Cecil Johnston was a U.S. Army captain and commander of Hdqrs. Co., 4th Armored Division, in this photo of him at his desk, probably in Geoppinger, Germany in the 1950s.

Inez Johnston and their children, Patricia and William at ice-covered Lake Eihsee near Garmish, Bavaria in March 1958

Family photo of Cecil and Inez Johnston and their
young children, Patricia and William, about 1958.

Capt. Cecil Johnston during his service in the 1950s occupation
of Germany. He received a battlefield commission from Gen.
George S. Patton and a battlefield promotion soon after from
Gen. Mark Clark during fierce WWII fighting to free Italy.

CHAPTER FIVE

"War Is Hell"

When Pearl Harbor happened, Cecil Johnston was on active duty with Company A, 179th Infantry Regiment of Oklahoma's famed 45th Division, stationed at a military base in Abilene, Texas.

It was early in 1941 when his National Guard unit was mobilized. "As soon as we got our feet on the ground, they moved us to Abilene.

"When we heard that Pearl Harbor had been attacked, all of us felt like, well, now we understand why we've been called up," Johnston said, much more than a half-century later.

Johnston was a 20-year-old "private in the rear ranks," when his Guard unit was mobilized.

After a battlefield commission from Gen. George S. Patton, a battlefield promotion from Gen. Mark Clark six months later, four Bronze Stars, a commendation ribbon with metal pendant and a stack of other awards for meritorious World War II action in North Africa, Sicily, Italy and elsewhere in Europe, Johnston retired from the Army as a major almost 21 years later.

He probably would have brought home a Purple Heart or two had he thought battlefield shrapnel wounds he received several times were serious enough to seek medical attention.

Johnston was discharged with a 60 percent service-connected disability that had caused him to be shell shocked.

He also learned from a medical specialist many years later, that he had suffered a broken back during the heavy World War II fighting to gain a foothold in Italy.

Johnston decided when the war was over to reenlist in the Army and saw more than a decade of service with the U.S. occupation forces in Germany and Japan.

"I said, I've given the best years of my life; might as well stay around for 20 years."

In that spring of 1941, Johnston's company was first sent to Fort Sill, Oklahoma where "training was pretty primitive," he remembers. "People don't realize what we went through in World War II."

On their arrival, "we had to make our own place to stay" at Fort Sill. "I was dragging dirt around in a toe sack to make a pad," first for pup tents, later for square, four-man tents.

"I guess they were toughening us up for what we'd be doing in the real war."

At one point, they marched 60 miles in 52 hours without stopping, with full field packs. Then they marched from Abilene, in west Texas to Fort Polk in west central Louisiana.

"We camped when we got there," Johnston said. "We would walk all day, then camp at night. The next morning, if we were lucky, there would be a truck for us to ride in for a few hours, then we would march. We would walk one day, maybe get to ride a little bit the next day, then march some more the next.

"We made it. Some men fell out and would have to be picked up by an ambulance. But not many.

"All of us were ole' country boys. We did what we thought we were supposed to do."

When they were first mobilized, they were formed into four regiments. After Pearl Harbor was attacked, one regiment was pulled out to be sent to the Pacific Theatre. Johnston was supply sergeant by then and it was his job to get them combat ready in three days.

He did it.

That regiment's departure, however, left his organization a triangle division: two regiments to serve on the front lines, one in reserve.

The company's first military action was in North Africa in June 1943. "That was what began the liberation of Europe," Johnston said.

North Africa was "sandy. No good." German Gen. Erwin Rommel against whom they were fighting, "was a really, really good general," Johnston said.

"War is hell. It's not fun. But it's a necessary evil sometimes," he mused.

From North Africa they battled their way through Sicily and Italy, through small arms fire, artillery fire, hails of shells.

"The 45th Division spent more days on the front lines than any other unit of the Army," Johnston said, "something like 500 days.

"We didn't get to go home after 30 days, or a year, because this was World War II. We were on the front lines longer than any other combat organization. I saw an awful lot of friends go down."

One of the Bronze Stars he received was for infantry combat action in the amphibious landing on Sicily. Johnston's first lieutenant went down, hit by small arms fire from three sources.

But mention of that brought back one of his worst memories: when his next lieutenant was hit by an .88 mm. shell from a German tank "and was blown all to pieces. I was right next to him."

The dead man "was a really nice officer," Johnston said.

It happened after the landing at Salerno, Italy. "That's where we lost the most troops. Nearly all our C Company."

Such memories never go away, Johnston said. "That's the reason we don't like to talk about it."

He tries to look on the brighter side. But he reminds listeners in Veterans Day talks that about a half million people gave their lives in World War II.

"That's a lot of people," he said.

What did he do to earn those Bronze Stars?

"Just lived," Johnston said.

One came from action as they fought their way across Sicily from a beach landing to its north side. When they got Sicily secured, they landed at Salerno and moved up the peninsula through such spots as Naples, Foggia, Rome, the Arno.

A second Bronze Star came from the fighting at Salerno. Johnston was knocked unconscious when the lieutenant standing next to him was blown to bits by the .88 shell.

He is sure that had to be when he suffered the severe back injury that an Oklahoma City back specialist in recent years told him he had received a long, long time ago, probably in the military.

"In a situation like that, kids like me said, 'we'll tough it out' and survived."

Another Bronze Star was from fighting "at a monastery where we had so many people killed."

Johnston was cut off from his unit for three days at a point between Naples and Rome. Officials listed him as killed in action.

It was at this period of Johnston's life that he made a covenant with God.

"I was cold, hungry, wet and had no idea what the Lord had in store for me," Johnston said.

On a rain-swept Italian mountaintop, in a region swarming with well-armed enemy, Johnston asked God "to help me get out of this," and made some promises of his own.

One of Johnston's pledges was to do the best he could to complete the mission.

"The Lord did his part and I am still trying to do my part of the covenant," Johnston said.

Recounting the monastery battle, Johnston said "the Germans came in. We fought our way back.

"We ran into a monastery; as we went through, we took everybody's weapons away from them. We treated the people nice but we took the weapons out of their hands."

When they reached the monastery, they found it was also filled with German and Italian soldiers.

"We shelled it and flattened it. We didn't ask nobody."

Johnston was awarded his battlefield commission from General Patton in Italy not long after he was cut off from his unit.

"Company C was annihilated yesterday," the general said, as he made Johnston a second lieutenant and pledged to rebuild the company.

"He sent me over there to find the people I could find. He sent more troops. I put them all together," Johnston said.

Patton "was one fantastic general. I thought the world of him because I had seen him in action. He was one of the few generals who were on the front line."

Another three-star general, Mark Clark, when Johnston got in his command, promoted him to first lieutenant. That was also in Italy, about six months later.

His fourth Bronze Star was awarded for meritorious service in World War II.

Johnston was in Sicily when he first had to shoot an enemy soldier at close range. "It was always hard," he said.

"I'd try to make them give up and take their stuff away from them so I wouldn't have to shoot them."

In Italy he captured a German full colonel whose plane had been shot down. Speaking perfect English, the colonel said, "get me out of here."

Johnston told him to "hunker down and stay with us. I wanted to be sure to get him back safely because they (U.S. Army officials) wanted to interrogate him. We weren't doing that; we were fighting a war."

They fought alongside the British, an American-Japanese regiment from California and Hawaii and also some Kurds.

The Japanese-Americans "were great soldiers," he said. "I've seen them walking on their dead to keep up with us."

The Kurds "were the most unique people I have ever seen-outstanding soldiers."

When the 45th was mobilized, "we got people from all walks of life; from New York" and elsewhere, he said.

Johnston, as a first sergeant, memorized 215 people's service numbers so if someone was killed, he would be able to supply a little more information than just the man's dog tags.

Bill Mauldin, the famous cartoonist who created the bearded, battle weary GIs, Joe and Willie, "used to come by my orderly room and get stories," Johnston said. "He was one of the nicest people I ever met. He was looking for information. He knew how to put a story together."

Johnston said Mauldin got the idea for Joe from the 45th. "If you didn't joke a little, it would kill you. This combat stuff will eat your lunch," he said.

CHAPTER SIX

The War Is Over!

They held the line in Italy, Johnston said, backing the enemy up into Germany. When the war in Europe was over in spring 1945, his company was sent into Germany as an occupation force but he remained in Italy about a year.

Johnston spent the rest of his 21 years of Army service in the occupation of mainly Germany but also Japan. He helped with the reconstruction of both countries.

That commendation ribbon with metal pendant from the Department of the Army was for his work after the war in moving about 17,000 troops and their dependents overseas to relieve a division that was on the front lines in Germany.

The Shawnee resident for nearly 50 years was anxious to learn as he went along. Johnston managed to see Mt. Vesuvius erupting outside Naples. "I wanted to be able to tell my grandchildren about it.

"Vesuvius was a unique thing. Hot lava, eight inches deep or more- burning fire and brimstone- coming down the mountain. When I saw Pompeii right under it, I said to myself, no wonder Pompeii was covered up."

When they were going through Rome, Johnston got to see Pope Pius XII.

"He blessed me and handed me rosary beads. He was being carried on the shoulders of some people. This was inside the Vatican.

"Here I am, a combat soldier with my uniform on.

"He didn't have to give a bunch of old dog-faced soldiers an audience just to recognize and bless you.

"He was, I thought, a very considerate and understanding individual."

After the war in Europe was over, Johnston was camp commander outside Naples and responsible for the general officers mess for perhaps a year.

Some of his soldiers were stealing the Italian people's *vino*- their wine. Johnston put a stop to that. The people urged him to go talk to the mother superior.

"We talked and visited. She spoke good English," Johnston said. She thanked him for coming over there and freeing them. "She was a very nice lady."

The sisters in her order "sewed my clothes so they were just like they were tailor-made." They gave him "little lace things they had made," as another gesture of appreciation.

After the war, he got to go to the Isle of Capri, made famous in song, and had lunch. "It looked real nice," Johnston remembers. "The boat went into a big cove in a rock formation. Inside, the water was clear as a crystal."

And, during the post-war occupation of Europe, "I built myself a sailboat. I supervised the Italians building it."

He got the biggest crane he could find but it wouldn't lift the finished boat, "but we did launch it."

He turned it over to a man who helped build it, when he left.

"I just saw so many things it's amazing. The Lord has been good to me, getting to see these things."

Years later, when he was again stationed in Europe, Johnston arranged for his children and grandchildren to go to Europe "to see some of these things" while he was there.

"We took all the kids to someplace in Europe- from Yugoslavia to the Netherlands, Austria or Switzerland."

When the entire war was over, a general tried to persuade Johnston to become a regular army officer. But when his time for discharge came, he wanted to get out of service.

Johnston came back to Shawnee in March 1946. He went to work as a butcher on East Main Street.

That same year, he and Inez Jones were married in Ada, Oklahoma.

Johnston's family knew the Jones family. A friend of his who was also just back from World War II service and attended the same church as Johnston, introduced them.

"I came home and told Mama I had found her daughter in law," Johnston recalled.

Inez Jones Johnston became the mother of his two children, Patricia Inez Johnston Derk and William Cecil Johnston.

In 2010, Patricia Derk and her husband, David Derk, lived in Tecumseh, Oklahoma, while William Cecil Johnston and his wife, Gay Johnston, resided in the McLoud, Oklahoma area. Derk died unexpectedly April 21, 2010, at their home.

Cecil Johnston worked until 1947 at the meat market on East Main. "I told Inez I think I'll go back in the service. I reenlisted and stayed until I retired in 1961. I was only out about one year."

He went back into the Army in 1947 as a master sergeant, the enlisted rank he had held before his battlefield commissions. But as time went by, Johnston's service to his country won him new promotions- to major by the time he retired.

He first went back to Fort Sill, then in February 1948 he was sent to Japan as part of the U.S. Army occupation.

After brief stops at Guam, Okinawa and Midway, Johnston was stationed at Yokohama, Japan, where he served for two years. Inez Johnston was allowed to accompany him on that overseas assignment.

In early 1948, Okinawa, which is part of Japan, "was torn up like jacks; all to pieces, shells of ships were still sticking up in the water. Even the ground was torn up," Johnston said.

On the Japanese mainland at that time, when Gen. Douglas MacArthur would go out on the streets, leaving Tokyo, "all the traffic stopped until he got by. Everybody saluted him. It was both for security and respect," Johnston remembers.

"In Japan, I think a lot of it was show. They have a long history of having dictators.

"They would bow down, whereas in Germany, they showed respect. They didn't bow down to anyone, Americans or any other occupation troops, but they showed respect."

Europe, immediately after the war, "was really torn up because we bombed their cities. Pieces of them were out in the street.

"But nobody had to have a sign saying this is France and this is Germany," Johnston continued. "When you drove out of Germany into France, it was dirty; I thought to myself, like the United States. But in Germany, everything was clean. Everybody took brooms and cleaned up their part of the street.

"If they ran into a big obstacle, I got the Army men and heavy equipment going and helped them clean it up.

"You'd go to the park and they'd do the same thing. They cleaned up everything."

The German people "weren't lazy," Johnston said. "They worked and that was why they were so hard to whip. They were well trained; very frugal and didn't waste anything.

"France was also bombed out but they didn't clean it up like the Germans did."

Johnston was a sergeant major in the communications battalion while in Japan.

He returned to the States in April 1950 for a two-year stay before being sent to Germany in September 1952 as part of the Army occupation there.

He was in Germany from '52 until September 1955. Then it was back to the U.S., until he was reassigned to Germany in December 1958. He remained in Germany that time until July 1960.

"In Washington, D.C., as soon as I got back to the States, somebody runs up a red flag and says, 'let's get that guy back overseas,' " Johnston quipped.

After Japan, Johnston was assigned to Fort Sam Houston, San Antonio, Texas. There, he was assistant G-4, logistics.

One of his jobs was "to keep the commissaries straight; inspect them." Another was to brief National Guard troops and assist with their training.

He conducted a separation point for people who were returning, but wanted to get out and not reenlist. For those retiring, he brought in Civil Service people to brief them.

Johnston also briefed funeral homes and people in service regarding funeral benefits available.

He reported how much money Fort Sam Houston, its personnel and their dependents spent in the community, "so they would realize we weren't deadbeats. A lot was public relations," Johnston said.

During that first two years back after the Japan service, the Johnstons' first child, their daughter Patricia, was born at Fort Sill April 28, 1951.

Their son William was born at Fort Polk, La., Jan. 6, 1957, while Johnston was in the U.S. overseeing a massive movement of troops and their dependents to Europe.

CHAPTER SEVEN

Moving a Little City Overseas

Soon after Johnston was sent to Germany in the early 1950s, he was handed a major role in moving some 17,000 troops and their dependents from Fort Hood, at Killeen,Texas, to a small town near Stuttgart, Germany.

The 12,000 Fourth Armored Division troops were to relieve soldiers who had served on the front lines during the war. The fresh troops were to serve in the U.S. occupation of Germany and help in the reconstruction of Europe.

Johnston had to have housing ready for them all, including the 5,000 or 6,000 dependents when they arrived.

No small job.

He was sent to Fort Polk to start the movement of the 17,000 being gyroscoped to Europe.

A one-star general was in charge: General Del Marr, whom Johnston described as "a very nice man; very professional and efficient." He was division commander of the advance party.

Johnston, by then a captain, was the head person for the G4 logistics. He was third in command of about four other people who were under Gen. Del Marr.

First the troops had to be moved to Fort Hood.

"They were going to go to Germany where the Army had personnel in a number of places. To get them from Fort Hood we had to ship out of New York.

"We were the advance party." Johnston was one of about 1,000 officers and enlisted men in the advance party.

"We had to find housing for all those people. We tried and tried to match up the number of people they were bringing in with the housing that was available."

The troops were to be scattered out, part to Nuremberg, Stuttgart and other towns in the area. "We had a hard time matching up the spouses and their families to the housing that was available in Europe, compared to what was available in the United States," he said.

"Like in Fort Hood, or Fort Polk in Louisiana, there were communities nearby for them to live in." Comparing the picture in Germany at that time to Oklahoma, Johnston said "over there, it would be more like having some in Tulsa, Oklahoma City and Muskogee, and some in Lawton."

Johnston remembers one night sitting at a table with the other officers at 1 a.m. as they were trying to find answers. "I made a joke, then we started getting down to the nitty-gritty and finally figured out what to do.

"When they got there we had it figured out where to put the dependents. That was one of the biggest jobs we had, trying to match the dependents in the locality where the servicemen were.

"But we had to make some adjustments before they got on the high seas so they'd have a place for them to go."

There were more problems when they got to New York. "We lost a lot of our people in New York. Some didn't have enough time (on their enlistments) to go to Germany and some didn't have good enough records. They were taking their dependents with them," he said.

Johnston said he had a lot of friends in the military. "I could go to Gen. Patton and talk to him."

Once during the massive troop moving project, "one of my generals told me, 'here's my pilot. He has my airplane. You go to USAEur (U.S. Army Europe Headquarters) and you know what I need. Don't come back until you get it.'

"I got it," Johnston said. "They were trying to get what they needed when they brought these 17,000 troops and dependents over there."

When he got to Headquarters, he was waiting at a table with 10 full colonels and a three-star general. "Here I was a lowly captain."

Johnston was sent to Goeppergan, Germany, when he went back.

He had plenty of work to do.

"Every year you had to pass your operational fitness test. I passed; it was as a captain in command of a company."

He recalls being asked to run the company of another man who was AWOL, and run it well so the AWOL man would get a good grade. "The man was a real well liked guy but I wouldn't do it."

Every year they had to go on maneuvers. "You wouldn't know when it was going to be," Johnston said, "but one night they would blow the whistle and you had to move out to a site and be combat ready."

Another of Johnston's responsibilities was to check the whole division for combat readiness.

"I was fortunate or unfortunate enough to be selected to be the one in the division to give a report on every unit and their combat readiness," Johnston said.

On one report he tried to be nice to a colonel, who was one of the unit commanders. But the general in charge told him to write it like it was. As a result, the colonel was relieved of his command.

"That was one of the hardest things I ever did because it was really a touchy situation.

"I never did figure I was a real fancy plutocrat. I was just an ole' country boy that Idaho Montana brought up teaching to do right," Johnston said.

"I really learned how the other half lived when that general put his plane and pilot at my disposal. Here I am, flying all over Germany in a plane that belongs to a one-star general. All the G-4s were full colonels or lieutenant colonels, and I was a captain."

Much of his work was administrative but his unit still had to be combat ready. When he mobilized his unit, Johnston told his general he was ready.

"The general said 'go to the border and act like you are going to attack.' But we didn't go over the border." Sometimes other people were doing the same thing on the other side

He also checked expenditures to be sure they were legally correct and came from the right funds. All the payrolls of civilian employees came to him from U.S. Army Europe to be checked.

He was once told he was the only one who could bail a general out who was spending money for salaries that was earmarked for something else.

Johnston asked who he was. He knew the man and agreed to give him money from his funds to make the general's expenditures right.

"But I never shorted my generals," he said.

Top brass military leaders were not the only VIPs with whom Johnston became closely acquainted during his tour of duty in post-war Germany in the early 1950s. He also became friends with Elvis Presley during that period.

Soon after he helped move the 17,000 troops and their dependents from Fort Hood to the little town near Stuttgart, then Capt. Johnston, picked up then Army Pvt. Elvis Presley at the railroad station in

Bad Nauheim, West Germany. Presley was standing on the depot platform with about a half-dozen other troops when they met.

"I asked him," Johnston recalled, "you're the famous singer, aren't you? I'll go to Public Relations and get you a job singing all over Europe.

"Elvis said, 'no sir. I want to serve my country on the front lines.'

"We were still in a combat mode," Johnston said. "We had an alert every month, in which we would move right up to the border of East Germany and Russia. This was about the height of the Cold War."

Once a month during the alerts, they quickly moved troops to the front lines, in combat ready position.

Presley was to be a driver for a commander. Since Johnston was a junior commander, he tried to arrange for him to be his driver but a colonel said no, Presley should drive a senior commander.

"Every time we had a meeting, I'd go over to him and talk to him," Johnston said. "We got to be good friends. He was world famous at that time- maybe not as much as later on, but very well known.

"Presley said, 'I'll go back and start my career again when I go home but right now, I want to serve my country.'

"He was just a real friendly guy and impressed me as being very intelligent, educated and well-informed. He talked about the world situation and could hold a conversation with you about whatever subject you wanted to talk about.

"He was a nice guy to talk to. Elvis got along good with all the other servicemen," Johnston remembers. They were together about 18 months to two years.

Johnston was in Germany twice as a member of the military for a total of four and one-half years in the 1950s.

He returned as a civilian for another four years in the first half of the 1980s, while employed at Tinker Air Force Base.

It was during that stay in Germany that he brought his children and grandchildren over to see Europe. Each one was shown a different country or area.

"When they opened Yugoslavia up, we were on the first bus that was allowed to go in there, and we went in from Germany. I had a ball," Johnston said.

"I got to see those white stallions that Gen. Patton had saved during World War II."

CHAPTER EIGHT

Back to Civilian Life- and Public Service

Cecil Johnston held the rank of major when he retired from the U.S. Army in April 1961.

He had risen from "private in the rear ranks," as he termed it, when his National Guard unit was mobilized in spring 1941, to first lieutenant following a battlefield commission and subsequent promotion for outstanding service during World War II fighting on the Italian war front.

He received an honorable discharge in March 1946, returned to Shawnee, Oklahoma, county seat of Pottawatomie County, his home county. He worked a year in a Shawnee meat market, and got married.

When he decided in 1947 to reenlist, he went back into the Army at the rank of sergeant, the position he held when Gen. Patton made him a second lieutenant on the Italian battlefield.

Johnston rose from sergeant to major in the succeeding 14 years of Army service.

When he retired from the Army in April 1961, he'd put in nearly 21 years of military service from the day he joined the Oklahoma National Guard in September or October 1939.

Johnston returned to Shawnee that April '61, and went to work for American National Insurance Company.

Dean Hudlow was his boss. "He taught me everything I know about insurance," Johnston said.

He also remembers, "I fought it all the way because I'm not a good salesman."

Johnston must have done a good job, however, because the company soon wanted to send him to Arkansas as the person in charge.

"I said no, but thanks. The Army has moved me for 20 odd years," Johnston said. He added that his wife wanted to stay in Shawnee.

"They tried to get me to stay but I left and got a job at the Post Office."

He was a letter carrier from September 1961-January 1962. But he was only allowed to work 20 hours per week.

So he applied at Tinker Air Force Base in Midwest City, Oklahoma, on the east edge of the Oklahoma City metroplex. Tinker was Pottawatomie County's largest employer for decades.

He passed the Civil Service test and qualified to be on the employee roster.

"The man doing the hiring and firing looked at me and said, 'you're an officer and you won't work.' I said, try me.

"We say that in the Masons. I found out later the man was a Mason and he recognized that phrase, 'try me.' "

He called Johnston back and told him two of his former supervisors had responded positively to his query about Johnston. Both called him "the best worker I've ever had."

"I started out at a lowly job," Johnston said. He was packaging things to ship out. But, "I came to work, did what I was supposed to do."

Johnston started work at Tinker at $1.78 per hour as a laborer.

When he retired 30 years later, he was a GS 11 annually administering at least $400 million for repair of aircraft engines; $200 million for maintenance of Air Force One and one other plane that was used by a four-star general in the Panama Canal area, plus another $100 million for repair of any engines on which they did not have a contract and other miscellaneous items.

As finance officer for maintenance of aircraft engines and Air Force One, Johnston made the decisions about fixing the problems that came in.

He was a laborer about a year "because I knew I had only 30 years to get up that ladder.

"I was thankful I had a job and was working every day and those people were nice to work with but I got promoted."

He became a supervisor of inspection, checking items and expenditures- making sure they were legally correct and coming out of the right funds.

In the mid-1960s, Shawnee Board of Education became embroiled in perhaps the worst financial crisis in its history.

The administration, apparently with board approval, was paying the school district's bills, including teachers' salaries, with non-payable warrants. The district's checks were good- teachers and vendors could cash them and get their money- but the practice meant borrowing money from the bank to cover their checks.

And banks charge interest to those to whom they lend money, even school districts. Basically, the district was running up big interest charges.

Johnston's job at Tinker Field involved checking that good money management practices were being followed.

He was also an active Shawnee Public School patron with a daughter entering high school and a son in the early years of elementary school.

So he was interested when he began reading newspaper reports about the non-payable warrants being issued.

Interested to the point that he went to the school administration building and asked, "would you mind telling me how you spend your money? How do you commit money and spend money?"

He was told "you don't need this information. None of your business," Johnston vividly remembers.

"I tried to be nice," Johnston said. He also told them, "I'll be back."

He had records that showed that $93,000 in interest on non-payable warrants had been paid by the school district.

"That was what I was asking about. That's not exactly the way the government let me do business."

Next time there was a vacancy on the school board, Johnston was appointed to fill it "because I was rocking the boat, in my opinion."

That was in 1966.

When he became a board member, Johnston made a motion that they do not issue any more non-payable warrants. The motion passed.

"That was the main axe I had to grind," he said, "to stop paying interest on taxpayers' money when all you had to do was manage your budget properly."

No criminal wrongdoing was involved.

"I was not saying what somebody was doing was wrong, nor mismanagement of funds. There was just a better way to do it" than paying interest on the warrants the district was issuing

"We looked for a better, less expensive way to do it," he said.

The late Bill Brokaw resigned as superintendent, however. Brokaw was highly regarded as a Shawnee school administrator who personally did much good for students during the difficult days of the Depression.

The board hired the late Don Owens to succeed him as superintendent. Owens later became an administrator at Cameron College, Lawton, Oklahoma.

At the appropriate time, Johnston won election to his school board seat. The opponent he defeated asked for a recount, but Johnston won it by about 25 votes.

He was elected to two four-year terms: 1967-75, and was president of the school board in 1974-75.

For the nine years Johnston was on the school board, the district did not issue another non-payable warrant, he said.

"It was probably an office manager who said it was none of my business," Johnston continued. "I had read about it in the paper. I wondered why they were in such trouble. I knew they had money because it was coming from the taxpayers.

"I think they have straightened out their act now because they're getting more money, but it's easy to be rote and do it the way they have been doing it," he said.

Another incident he recalls from his years on the mid-'60s through mid-'70s Shawnee Board of Education happened when the kitchen equipment at a school in the poorer part of town went out.

"They said, we'll put the new equipment in (the system's newest elementary school) and send (the newest school's) equipment down to (the poorer school).

"I said, 'no, we're not going to play that game.' We did it right and put it where it was supposed to go.

"I said, 'when the other one wears out, we'll get a new one for them.' It was more work to swap the equipment, and you're showing preferential treatment to the rich people" to do it any other way.

While he was on the board, they replaced all the equipment in all the school kitchens that was needed, "to try to get all of them up to date.

"We got the first computer-type equipment that was available, not all at the same time. We had to do it gradually but we got it all done."

The board also improved the system's playground equipment during his tenure, "because it was cheaper to buy in quantity if you can afford it. A lot of times you could afford it if you managed your money properly.

"I thought we as a team did a lot of things to help all the people in the community to where everybody got a fair shake. I worked with some nice people," Johnston said.

Two he particularly mentioned were Dr. Leon Westfall, who as Shawnee schools superintendent in the '70s, "was real good," and H. Jerrell Chesney, who was "supreme as vice-superintendent."

Chesney went on to become secretary of all the state higher education system, "and I helped write a letter to get him on that," Johnston said.

"It turned out Chesney was a really good secretary. I think he was the third highest paid person in state government.

"We had some good educators here in Shawnee. I got to work with them locally."

Johnston did not seek reelection to a third term because he was going to become worshipful master of Masonic Lodge No. 107, which had about 600 members.

The Shawnee News-Star ran a headline, "Johnston Quits," he remembers. "I didn't quit. I chose not to run," Johnston stated.

The News-Star reported a little later that the district had started issuing non-payable warrants again after Johnston left the board. "The next month after I was off, they started doing it again. That was 1975," Johnston said.

CHAPTER NINE

Never a Dull Moment

Soon after Johnston returned to Shawnee after retiring from the Army, he persuaded Draper Street United Methodist Church and the Boy Scouts of America's Last Frontier Council to let him start Boy Scout Troop, Post 403 at the church.

During his 17 years as scoutmaster, Johnston, aided by two assistant scoutmasters and the scouts' parents, saw 28 boys achieve Eagle rank.

Among them were his son, William C. Johnston; Dr. Mickey Sehorn, the late Dewayne Luton who became Oklahoma City Chamber of Commerce' youngest president; David Austin, Major Marvin Collier, Billy Collier, John Goodson, Rick Hill, Calvin Purkey, Ralph Brown and Barnard Cooper.

The troop went camping every month and to summer camp annually; floated down the Illinois River, a scenic waterway in eastern Oklahoma every spring; went to Fort Sill for two to five days several times; to Lake Darnell in Arkansas and observed state lawmakers in session at the state capitol each February.

Former longtime Shawnee High School principal Elmo Pipps once told Johnston he wished every boy could go through his troop.

Johnston won the Order of the Arrow Award on October 24, 1970. That award is given to an individual who spends a night alone in a wilderness area.

On February 20, 1973, Johnston received the Silver Beaver Award, the Last Frontier Council's highest award, at the same time the late veteran Congressman Tom Steed, Shawnee, was presented the honor.

Johnston calls his Boy Scout work one of the most rewarding things he's ever done.

Cecil Johnston's wife, Inez, was diagnosed with breast cancer about 1976. He had a small grandchild hanging onto his leg- his daughter's child whom he was baby sitting- when the doctor told him his wife could not live.

Inez Johnston died in November 1978 in Shawnee.

Louise Roark Johnston's first husband, the late Kenneth Roark, died before Inez Johnston's death.

She had been a widow about two years when she and Cecil Johnston became acquainted at St. Mark's United Methodist Church which they both attended.

"I drove up to her house on Center Street (in Shawnee) and asked her for a date," Johnston recalled.

Cecil and Louise Johnston were married Oct. 3, 1979, in Bonham, Texas.

"I inherited three children when Louise and I got married," he said. "They weren't adopted but they became my kids."

Anita Ruth Roark, 18, was still living at home and joined their household when her mother and Cecil Johnston were married. His new sons were Bert Roark who was 22, and Richard Roark, 21 at that time. Bert Roark now lives in San Bernardino, California, and Richard Roark in Bartlesville, Oklahoma. Anita Ruth Roark lives in Shawnee.

Johnston's son William was also living at home when they married.

Cecil and Louise Johnston's blended family now includes eight grandchildren.

The couple observed their 30th wedding anniversary in October 2009.

Johnston has said he was "fortunate to have two wonderful wives." The first, the late Inez Johnston, died after 32 years of marriage. "Then I found Louise," he said.

Johnston was elected to the Ward 4 seat of Shawnee City Commission on May 5, 1980.

"Louise told the two kids who were at home (William Johnston and Anita Ruth Roark) that I was going to run for city commissioner," he remembers.

She told them there would be a lot of phone calls even on Saturdays and Sundays, from people wanting him to do things for them, etc. "The pressure that's going to be on you is not going to be easy," she warned. "Don't get any traffic tickets," Louise Johnston added.

"In six months they'd both moved out," Cecil Johnston said.

He served as Ward 4 commissioner until October 1981, when Tinker Air Force Base officials sent him to Germany as a civilian employee.

Johnston's service during that 17 months on the City Commission plus four more years he served as Ward 6 commissioner after his return from Europe will be described in a later chapter.

Johnston quips that he "went to prison" when he got to Germany.

He did, sort of. Except he was an official, not a prisoner.

Johnston became finance officer for the U.S. Army confinement facility in Mannheim, Germany.

It housed Army, Air Force and Navy prisoners, "although they seldom got anyone from the Navy," he said.

"Louise was scared to death to go in there," Johnston said, explaining that his office was in the prison.

Petty theft was the main offense, along with charges such as assault.

"But some were in there for murder," Johnston said.

He recalls filling out an income tax return for a female sergeant who was an inmate.

Johnston asked her marital status on the preceding Dec. 31. "Married," she replied. "Are you filing jointly?" he asked. The husband was deceased, Johnston learned.

"I killed him," she said.

The woman was later convicted and sent to a federal prison in the United States.

"In that prison, you saw all kinds of things," Johnston said. "One guy tried to rape the chaplain's secretary.

"Never a dull moment."

Johnston was prison finance officer until he got promoted. "Man, was I working hard to get a promotion!"

He became finance officer for an Army regiment, a division, in charge of handling all its finances and training.

Sometimes he would handle a combat command. On occasion, Johnston would rent entire villages for Army uses.

"Never a dull moment" there, either.

In the finance officer position, he was headquartered in Frankfurt.

While there, Johnston completed work toward a bachelor's degree in business administration at a European branch of the University of Maryland.

It was located in Heidelberg, in the largest building in Europe.

Johnston had previously done some college work at the University of Oklahoma, Louisiana State University and a university in Japan.

He had tried to earn college credits wherever there was an opportunity to do so.

He interested Louise Johnston in completing her college work at the University of Maryland, too, and they both received their bachelor degrees at the same time: May 7, 1984.

A two-star general who knew Johnston from his earlier Army service, wanted to present him his diploma, and did so during the University of Maryland's commencement ceremonies in the officers club within the large Heidelberg building.

For the commencement, they had to have tents outside for people to put on their caps and gowns to prepare for the upcoming activities. "It was such a big affair, the biggest building in Europe couldn't accommodate all the people," Johnston said.

"All the work I did on getting my college degree helped me later with better managing my time," Johnston said. He was 64 when he graduated.

While in Germany as a civilian government employee, Johnston showed Louise Johnston's children and her mother points in Europe.

He was assigned to a five-year tour of duty in Europe but in mid-1985, four years into the tour, his mother made several trans-Atlantic telephone calls to him.

"I knew that Indian lady wouldn't be calling if everything was alright," Johnston said.

He and his wife came back to Shawnee one year early- in September 1985- because he had a distinct feeling, deep down, that his mother needed him.

She did.

Idaho Montana Johnston died Dec. 11, 1985. She was 85.

"If I had to name the one person who was the greatest influence on my life, I would say Idaho Montana Johnston," Cecil Johnston said many years later.

When he returned to work at Tinker Air Force Base, Johnston became finance officer for engines and Air Force One and miscellaneous aircraft maintenance.

That was when Johnston, who started at the Oklahoma City area Air Force base as a laborer in early 1962, became responsible for handling those multi-million dollar budgets.

He successfully accomplished that work until he retired from Tinker in 1992.

Louise Johnston worked almost 30 years at Tinker, retiring about a year after he did.

But Cecil Johnston wasn't through working.

He was employed eight more years by Shawnee attorney Kermit Milburn as trust fund manager. His official designation was president of the trust fund.

Johnston retired from that position in 2000.

Johnston in his fez hat as a Shrine Club member during the late 1960s. He made kids laugh and adults smile while driving a midget Shrine Club car in parades throughout the area. Johnston returned to Shawnee and civilian life in 1961.

Cecil Johnston, as he was completing service as president of Shawnee Board of Education and was employed at Tinker Air Force Base, about 1975.

Louise Roark Johnston was a widow when she and
widower Cecil Johnston were married in October 1979.
Her daughter, Anita Ruth Roark, and his son, William
Johnston, with them in this 1979 photo, moved in with the
newly married couple, but both soon moved out after Cecil
Johnston was elected to Shawnee City Commission.

Back again in Germany, this time as a civilian employee
of Tinker AFB, Johnston is shown trying to get his
BMW moving on a snowy day in the early 1980s.

Cecil and Louise Johnston about 1985, soon after their return to Shawnee from Germany.

Louise Johnston's children, Anita Ruth Roark, Bert Roark, and Richard Roark, whom Cecil Johnston says "weren't adopted but became my kids" when the couple married.

4B   The Shawnee News-Star, Sunday, September 11, 1994

MILESTONE REACHED — American Legion   in American Legion Post 16 to W.D. Collins, right.
Commander Cecil Johnston, left, presents a   Franklin Gray, not pictured, also received a 50-
framed certificate honoring 50 years membership   year certificate. (Staff photo by Ed Blochowiak)

Cecil Johnston, (left) commander of American Legion Post 16, Shawnee, presents 50-year membership certificate to W.D. Collins in September 1994. Photo courtesy of Staff Photographer Ed Blochowiak and the Shawnee News-Star.

Cecil Johnston driving a four-wheeler towing a float
depicting a sailboat as Shawnee Twin Lakes Association's
entry in a Shawnee parade about 2004 or '05.

Cecil Johnston, (left), receives 2006-07 C.T. Bush Most Valuable
Lt. Governor Award from William E."Bill"Crump III, past
Texas-Oklahoma Kiwanis District governor. Johnston was
selected from more than 40 lieutenant governors serving with
Crump in 2006-07. Photo courtesy of Gary Hicks, editor, and
Ki-Notes, Texas-Oklahoma Kiwanis District publication.

CHAPTER TEN

Helping Run the City of Shawnee

Cecil Johnston was elected to a second term on Shawnee City Commission- and a first term as Ward 6 commissioner- May 5, 1986, about eight months after his return from his European mission for Tinker Air Force Base.

He won the Shawnee Ward 4 seat on the Commission May 5, 1980, but had to resign from the position when Tinker officials assigned him to a five-year tour of duty in Germany in 1981.

Johnston came back in September 1985, however, to check on his mother's health.

People approached Johnston urging him to run for city commissioner prior to his elections to those two seats. He had already served nine years on Shawnee Board of Education.

With each job, there were changes in city manager or school superintendent "and this meant you had to hire somebody" to take the outgoing administrator's place.

"So you interviewed and made a decision. Some of them were hard decisions, some weren't," Johnston said.

"All of them were very time consuming and you had to really really try your best" to make a wise decision.

"You had to do your own research," he continued. Johnston said he has called people in the communities where the candidates were from, "to help me make up my mind.

"You meet nice people. You had the same thing on the City Commission (as on school board) except in a different aspect."

One of the main things he remembers from his years on City Commission was, "we changed city managers two or three times while I was in there."

City staff "kept their money pretty straight," Johnston found, and "the city was better managed overall than I thought it would be.

"But when it's changing hands, things get disclosed but you don't notice it. Everybody is entitled to have their own ideas about how to get things done.

"I thought our city managers were pretty good," Johnston said. "Some were better than others.

"Jim Hudgens, I thought, was one of the better ones. He had been a policeman. He knew the problems of the police department.

"He was an honest, down-to-earth individual," Johnston said.

"I thought there was no skullduggery or lack of proper management" during Hudgens' administration, he added.

Johnston was off the commission when Hudgens was fired during a late night commission meeting in the early '90s.

He had been city manager at Sallisaw, Oklahoma when he took the Shawnee job. After his abrupt dismissal, he returned to Sallisaw, again became its city manager and held that position until he retired years later.

Among other decisions that had to be made during Johnston's terms on City Commission:

"We had administrative things that would happen. We talked about salaries. One of the first things I did was to move to increase the salaries of the city employees," Johnston said.

He was successful in that effort.

"We talked about the streets; we talked about the airport; pros and cons of the Expo Center.

"Maintenance of the streets was a big expenditure. We had a program geared to providing funds so you could fix so many streets each year" through the third penny sales tax.

"I had to learn what the Expo Center did. I found that it brought in a lot of people to this community. I said, 'that's good. If they bring in new people, maybe they'll come back to our community.' "

He remembers a problem arose at the airport when it developed that some contaminants had been left that had not been disposed of properly.

Another issue concerned benefits the country club was apparently receiving.

"I had to do a lot of digging to find out that they were getting water and not paying for it.

"I thought, why are people in the country club who've got money, getting things that we peons don't get?

"I prefer doing things by sitting down and talking to people," and doing it as quietly as possible, Johnston said. "We had some closed door meetings."

There were totally different situations to deal with during his years on the school board and City Commission but he believes he saw preferential treatment in both places.

Johnston supported getting the Senior Citizens Center built at 401 N. Bell. He voted to give $25,000 in city funds to get it started.

The center was created in space converted from a women's basketball dressing room and shower on the east side of Municipal Auditorium. A flanking men's dressing room on the auditorium's west side was converted to offices for Central Oklahoma Economic Development District (COEDD).

"Both are still in existence," Johnston said. "It took more than $25,000 but that was what got it started."

That action was during his first term.

The late Don Bodard, his friend from Earlsboro school days, came to Johnston one day and said he wanted to build Shawnee a new public library.

"He said he had talked to the city manager about it but everybody put him on hold," Johnston said.

"I have already committed myself to the IRS," Bodard told Johnston, showing him where he had reported putting $125,000 in on the proposed project.

"I need to be doing something to earn this; to build the library. This is something they have already agreed to," the oil man, later a wealthy banker, said.

Johnston went to Gene Rainbolt, the president of the other Shawnee bank who had brought in the city's then-new northside industries.

"Mr. Rainbolt said, 'I'll be glad to help you because we need a library.' With his help and my pushing on the City Commission, Don Bodard came in and did what he wanted to do: build a new library," Johnston said.

It was a $1 million or more facility that is still serving Shawnee citizens well.

Johnston said he learned much from trips ranging from Washington, D.C. to Las Vegas, Nevada, that the Commission made to attend conferences on various municipal government-related subjects.

"At each place they would have people setting up things for the cities. One was about cities with old, worn-out sewers and how you could replace them by telescoping them to help strengthen them."

Johnston said he learned numerous things that to him, were unique.

"I always came back and turned in a report about what I did with my time and what I gained from it because the taxpayers paid to send us.

"Once I tried to pay back $100 but they wouldn't let me, because they didn't want to start a precedent," Johnston said.

While he had previously been to most of the cities visited, "I met a lot of nice people and learned a lot of things. We went to D.C. a couple of times, Boston, Las Vegas, Atlanta," and elsewhere.

Johnston sought reelection in 1990, but lost "because I got crossways with political opponents and didn't get enough votes. But I'm not upset with nobody.

"I just thank the good Lord that I had an opportunity to serve both the city of Shawnee and on the school board and I feel like I provided a positive approach to doing those things.

"I learned a lot from both of them and tried not to hurt too many people's feelings," Johnston said.

"I loved every day on the City Commission and the school board. There were all kinds of opportunities to do good for the city and the school system."

He had considerable prior experience, having lived in places ranging from Okinawa and Japan to North Africa, Italy, Germany, Greece and Switzerland, in addition to many years in Shawnee as a taxpayer and school patron.

Both Shawnee City Commission and Board of Education positions, although involving long hours' work, were unpaid jobs.

CHAPTER ELEVEN

From Old Folks' Meals to Youth Rodeo Help

Cecil Johnston made a covenant with God on an Italian mountaintop during World War II at a time he says he was "cold, hungry, wet and had no idea what the Lord had in store for me."

Asking the Lord to "help me get out of this," Johnston said, "I agreed to do the best I could with His help to complete the mission and do the best I could to be a good ambassador for Him and His kingdom here on earth.

"The Lord did His part and I am still trying to do my part of the covenant," Johnston, at age 89, said in spring 2010.

That's why Johnston is still delivering hot lunches "to the old folks" as he terms it, just as he has done almost since the inception of the Meals on Wheels program.

It's also why for years he regularly drove veterans from Shawnee, Earlsboro, Bethel, Seminole and Prague, Oklahoma, to the Veterans Administration hospital in Oklahoma City;

Led a Boy Scout troop that graduated 28 Eagle Scouts;

Taught defensive driving classes for over 20 years, resigning in 2009 because of declining eyesight;

Worked hard to get enlisted men and non-commissioned officers the biggest pay raise they'd had in years;

Served two terms on Shawnee City Commission, nine years on Shawnee Board of Education including one as board president, and two terms on the Oklahoma State School Board Association;

Prepared low income people's income tax returns at no charge for 30 years;

Has met every Tuesday for five years with a committee planning an Oklahoma Veterans Memorial Park in Shawnee to honor approximately 5,000 to 6,000 Oklahoma veterans who gave their lives for their country, going back to Spanish-American War days; and other state veterans of the nation's wars who also served;

Has been a member of East Central Workforce Investment Board for 10 years, a group dedicated to providing education opportunities to high school graduates and students, homeless people, the unemployed and other adults with severe financial problems;

Has served his St. Mark's United Methodist Church in every lay capacity from Sunday school teacher to chairman of its administrative board, member of trustees and voting delegate to the annual state conference, the latter three positions he still held in 2010;

Is licensed by the Oklahoma Conference of United Methodist Churches as a lay speaker and has filled pulpits at Maud, Bethel, McLoud, Tecumseh and St. Mark's in Shawnee numerous times;

Started, with his wife Louise, monthly bean suppers at St. Mark's to raise funds for local and extended church missions;

Started Gill-Mattox American Legion Post 16's annual program recognizing outstanding law enforcement officers, firefighters, educators and a soldier of the year;

Made kids laugh and adults smile in one of the Shrine Club's comic little cars in parades over the state;

Started an annual Memorial Day observance at Resthaven Cemetery east of Shawnee when he was Legion post commander;

One year, the Johnstons alone placed more than 1,000 flags on veterans' graves in Resthaven, Calvary Cemetery on U.S. 177 west of Shawnee, and at Sacred Heart Catholic Church Cemetery near Konawa, Oklahoma;

Was among supporters at the earliest organizational meetings aimed at creating Gordon Cooper Vocational-Technical School, now Gordon Cooper Technology Center;

With Louise Johnston, volunteered four summers at Shawnee's Heart of Oklahoma Exposition Center rodeos- including all three years of the National High School Finals Rodeo's run at Expo Center- plus a large RV rally.

And much, much more, nearly all while holding a full-time job, caring for a family and serving in leadership positions in civic, patriotic and fraternal organizations.

When he came down from that cold, rainy mountaintop, Johnston worked so hard at his part in trying to win the war that he received one battlefield commission and six months later, a battlefield promotion.

When the war was over, he reenlisted and gave 14 more years of his life to the U.S. Army occupation and reconstruction efforts in Europe and Japan.

"When I came back to civilian life, I felt I must give something back," Johnston said. "My children were going to school here, my family was here.

"You can't take and take and not give something back. I hope I've tried to do this."

The first community service project he undertook was organizing Boy Scout Troop 403 at Draper Street Methodist Church, at Tenth and Draper, Shawnee. Johnston devoted 17 years to that work and helped 28 boys achieve Eagle Scout rank.

Johnston calls that work one of the most rewarding things he's done. Delivering Meals on Wheels lunches, which he still does, and driving veterans to the VA hospital are also at the top of his list of "very worthwhile" activities.

His nine years on the school board started not long after his return to Shawnee. He was a member of the state school board association in 1966-67 and 1968-69.

People later encouraged Johnston to run for City Commission. "I enjoyed it," he said of his public service.

"On the school board, I felt like I got an education. On the City Commission, I learned a whole lot more."

During and before his school board years, Johnston was a member of the Masonic Lodge in Shawnee. When he was about to become worshipful master, the lodge's chief executive officer, Johnston did not seek reelection to the Board of Education.

Instead, he promised fellow members he would concentrate entirely on their organization's activities during his year as worshipful master.

Next he worked in the York Rite, progressing through Council, Chapter and Knights Templar, achieving Knight York Cross of Honor, its highest award.

Johnston then went to the McAlester Consistery where he taught and was in degree work with Knights Chapter Cross of Honor. "That was fun," he said.

Johnston's next step was to become a Shrine Club member. "You have to go through either York Rite or the Consistery" to be a Shriner, he explained.

He started going to parades all over Oklahoma, entertaining crowds with his little car.

Johnston was president of the Shawnee Shrine Club "at least twice." He remembers the late District Judge J. Knox Byrum succeeded him as president.

Johnston's Shrine activities were about 1967-70. After that, he entered National Sojourners Chapter 43, Tinker Air Force Base, is still active in it and is a life member.

"What we stress is preparedness of the country to protect all of our people," Johnston said. "In the beginning it was all (military) officers and warrant officers. Then they dropped it down to senior non-commissioned officers."

Instructing children and adults in flag history and respect is another of the Sojourners' areas of concern.

Johnston worked hard to get the pay raises for enlisted men and non-coms "because I had seen sergeants who were on welfare because their salaries were so small.

"Some were too proud for welfare but they qualified.

"I felt like I was obligated, having just retired, to try to help benefit their livelihood. They were entitled to it," Johnston said.

It was about this period, around 1968, that he attended a meeting at the Aldridge Hotel in Shawnee, chaired by the late Dr. John Bruton, organizer, founder and first superintendent of Shawnee's Gordon Cooper Vo-Tech School, now Gordon Cooper Technology Center.

He attended later such meetings, but recalls that was the first one.

"Working at Tinker, I said, 'shoot, man, yes! We need people for maintenance of aircraft and other technical things that vocational schools teach.'

"I went to the meetings until everything was pushing forward; until I saw it was going to happen."

Johnston is a life member of the American Legion, Veterans of Foreign Wars and Disabled American Veterans. He's also a member of 40 et 8 "which got its name in World War I from 40 soldiers and eight mules fitting in a boxcar."

He started the Legion's program of proper disposal of worn-out American flags.

Johnston said it was probably in the early 1970s when he started driving veterans to the VA hospital He did that at least five years.

Johnston worked in the Volunteer Income Tax Assistance (VITA) program about 30 years in Europe, Tinker AFB, Fort Sill and Shawnee. Johnston figured income tax returns for military personnel and civilians who wanted it, including inmates in the military prison in which he was finance officer in Germany.

He annually attended an Internal Revenue Service school for a week before each tax period.

"We were not required to do returns for people who had extremely large incomes. Primarily it was for low income people."

When he was working at Tinker, the IRS normally brought in someone from the Oklahoma Tax Commission to update VITA tax preparers on state income tax law.

Johnston recalls one such authority "was so good I wrote a letter to the Oklahoma City IRS headquarters and told them this man was a really good instructor, got his point across and listeners felt invigorated to do much more because of him.

"I forgot about it until one day, someone yelled across the street and said, 'hey Cecil, your letter got me a cash award!' "

Through the experience he gained during all those years, Johnston was able to help many people. One was an "old, old man who lived in the boonies in an old, old house."

Johnston found he had paid too much tax the year before, although he had employed an attorney to prepare his return. Johnston filed a revised form for him, the elderly man got a nice refund back and "was so thrilled. He couldn't believe it!"

He taught about 200 defensive driving classes during a period of 20 years or more for AARP and the Oklahoma Department of Public Safety.

Johnston was assistant state coordinator and instructor for District 8 which included Pottawatomie, Lincoln, Seminole, Hughes and Okfuskee Counties of Oklahoma.

Among his hundreds of students over the years was a Gordon Cooper Technology Center superintendent who attended one of his Chandler class sessions.

Johnston resigned from the defensive driving program in 2008 or 2009 and had to drop his VITA work after being diagnosed with macular degeneration that was impairing his eyesight.

Many of these service projects were happening simultaneously.

He started delivering lunches to the homebound at Horace Mann Elementary School before 1992 or so when Meals on Wheels was fully organized.

The Horace Mann program "was just a small one then; the PTA would supply names of people who were homebound in their school district."

Meals from the school cafeteria were taken out into the community.

Then Johnston got involved with the city-wide Meals on Wheels program now a part of Central Oklahoma Community Action program. Unity Hospital, Shawnee, provides special diet lunches while larger churches supply regular meals.

He's done that for about 20 years and in 2010 is still delivering hot lunches on two routes, "to six or seven old people," he said. "If I don't do anything but make them smile, I feel like it's been worthwhile."

When he started, his deliveries included anywhere from 11 to 17 people, he said.

Johnston started the American Legion's program recognizing outstanding people in the late 1990s or early 2000s. He was Legion post commander about 1997.

That was also when he started the Memorial Day program at Resthaven Cemetery. He told the history of the observance: how

Southerners started it as Decoration Day and how it developed into today's programs.

The Shawnee VFW post is responsible for placing flags on veterans' graves in Shawnee's Fairview Cemetery and Johnston has been speaker at their Memorial Day observances.

The St. Mark's bean supper proceeds benefit local and extended church missions and community projects such as Habitat for Humanity, Food Closet, a free health clinic and an Indian mission in eastern Oklahoma.

Johnston joined the Kiwanis Club about 1985 or so. He was invited by a boss at Tinker. Johnston checked out the main civic clubs and found Kiwanis was "the only one that had anything about honoring God." He decided to go with Kiwanis "because of that and because the man who asked me was my boss."

He began as a member of the noonday Kiwanis Club in Shawnee, built a new evening club because he was working days out of town, and later joined the Diamond K chapter in Shawnee which meets at 8:30 a.m.

Johnston was its president and secretary.

He became Kiwanis lieutenant governor in 1996-97 and in 2006-07.

During that first term, Johnston was honored as Distinguished Lt. Governor. The second time, he was named Most Distinguished Lt. Governor of Oklahoma-Texas.

"I was 86 or 87 years old at that time. I built the new club with the help of Roy Brizzell, (Kiwanis) governor of Oklahoma-Texas. It died a natural death."

Brizzell was from the Nicoma Park, Oklahoma area.

Johnston also built a club in Tecumseh. "It lasted a good while but is also defunct.

"I've tried to be a builder, not a tearer-downer," Johnston said.

He was president of the Pottawatomie County Historical Society; and has been a member of Greater Shawnee Area Chamber of Commerce for a number of years.

Johnston has received numerous awards and honors. One was a meritorious award presented to him for successfully moving those 17,000 Army troops and their dependents from Fort Hood to Germany and finding housing for them.

He received that award from a general "who didn't give things like that. But he said he was honoring me because it was such a distinguished accomplishment," Johnston said.

"I have lots and lots of beautiful memories of these things. If you feel like you have done something that helps mankind" you've succeeded, he said. "I've had such a good life and I thank the good Lord all the time."

CHAPTER TWELVE

Reflections from a Long, Full Life

Reflecting on his experiences, people he's known, things he's witnessed and some of the lessons he's learned along the way, one sunny spring day as his 90th birthday drew closer, retired U.S. Army Maj. Cecil Johnston credited his Grandpa Smith with having a big influence on his life.

"Grandpa Smith had a big influence through his work habits," Johnston said.

"He taught me how to fish, make cross ties to sell to the railroad, cut down trees so they would fall where you want 'em to.

"He'd say, 'pull your own weight. Don't expect somebody else to carry it.'

"Idaho Montana Johnston had a big impact on my life," he continued.

"Always a stable individual, she helped me cope with all the problems in life. My mama and my daddy Arthur, they both had an impact."

Several educators also immediately came to mind.

"Especially Cliff Tinkle in Earlsboro.

"He taught me math and how to use it. One of the things he told me was don't buy it if you can't pay for it. I've always tried to do that: if you can't afford it, don't buy it."

Johnston remembers coming back from the Army and hearing a friend tell how his son was having trouble with mathematics in college. Johnston recommended that his friend contact Tinkle.

"He came back and said after Tinkle had tutored him for about a week, his son didn't have any more math problems.

"And I would be amiss not to mention Bruce Jenkins in the educators. He was also in Earlsboro. I respected him; he was a good teacher. I would always go by and see him as I was coming back and forth here."

His Earlsboro High School basketball coach Earl Cole "was a good coach, special in the coaching business and in handling players, in my books," Johnston said. "He was a really, really nice man."

And there was Juanita Garner, an English teacher at Earlsboro High School he remembers, too. "She said I murdered the English language. I got my lessons, but I didn't express them exactly the way she wanted. She didn't flunk me. I didn't make A's but she tolerated me even if I wasn't the best English student she'd ever had."

A number of fine educators had a strong influence on Johnston in later years.

Elmo Pipps was principal of Shawnee High School and Horace Mann elementary school in Shawnee. Johnston still remembers Pipps' statement that he "wished every boy could go through Johnston's Boy Scout Troop," and other complimentary comments he made regarding the boys of his Post 403.

Pipps, a veteran of World War II action in the South Pacific, served as a gunner on a bomber, was wounded, and after his release from a hospital, was sent back to his organization for further service.

"He was not only a hero in World War II, but also in education in Shawnee and Pottawatomie County for many years," Johnston said.

He listed H. Jerrell Chesney, assistant superintendent of Shawnee Public Schools, as having an impact on his life, "especially during the nine years I was on the school board" during the 1960s through 1975.

"And Dr. Leon Westfall. He had a lot of impact on me. I thought he was an honest individual, very smart, in my books."

Dr. Westfall was a Shawnee superintendent of schools during the period Johnston was a Board of Education member.

Near the top of the list of people who influenced his life was Harry W. Hughes, a University of Oklahoma professor who was his company commander in World War II.

"He set examples for me on how to live life, I thought," Johnston said.

Don't make excuses. Produce. That was Hughes' advice.

"Others may have said sort of the same thing, but he came across to me most."

One other educator also immediately came to mind: Dr. Hartmut Schwarzkopf, an instructor in the education department of the University of Maryland-Europe. "He had a big impact on my life in numerous ways. He was a unique person," Johnston said.

Gen. George F. Patton was very high on his list.

"When he talked to us and told us Hannibal was in the same spot where we were standing, it made me think about it.

"He was trying to get elephants across the Alps and we've got tanks we're trying to get across the Alps, Patton told us. I had read about that in history.

"You and I know we didn't get tanks across the Alps, but it impressed me, a kid out of high school.

"He gave me a battlefield commission. Another general gave me a battlefield promotion but Gen. Patton was the impressive one."

Johnston remembers other, particularly outstanding military leaders, too.

"General Marshall was probably the smartest individual I ever heard talk. He was a really smart man in my books. He laid it out: why we're here, what we're going to accomplish and we're going to treat the people fairly, regardless. I thought it was a very impressive message I heard in North Africa.

"I learned so much going overseas in World War II."

Turning again to family, Johnston said his first wife, Inez, with whom he lived for 32 years, "was a very stabilizing and loving lady that took care of our two kids, Patricia Inez and William Cecil.

"And then (after her death) I was lucky to find another lady who was strong and supportive and that was Louise- and I gained three new children, Bert F. Roark, Richard Roark and Anita Roark.

"They all had an impact on me, too."

Turning back to memories of his experiences in the Oklahoma oil boom town of Earlsboro, Johnston could not forget the Rev. Argus Hamilton Sr., pastor of the Earlsboro Methodist Church when Johnston was a teenager.

"He had enough influence on me that I gave my heart to God and was saved," Johnston said.

"I was baptized in the Baptist church in Earlsboro because my Grandma Smith wanted me to be submerged and in the Methodist Church, they sprinkle," he recalled. (Mrs. Smith's husband was the grandfather who was a bootlegger in Oklahoma's Prohibition days.)

The minister "had enough influence on me," Johnston said, "to cause me to take music lessons and learn to play the piano well enough to play for the Sunday school and the Sunday night youth services."

Johnston was 16 or 17 years old and playing Earlsboro High School basketball at the time. His piano teacher was the high school music teacher.

Rev. Hamilton's son, Argus Hamilton Jr., was also a member of the Earlsboro basketball team. He and Johnston were close friends.

"He would come over to our house to sleep. We played basketball together, ran around together when we had time; did chores together."

Years later, Argus Hamilton Jr.'s son, Argus Hamilton III became famous as a comedian on national television. "He was on the nighttime shows. I didn't know him but I did know his daddy," Johnston said.

When he and Argus Hamilton Jr. wanted to go to the movies in Shawnee, Johnston's father would tell them they could take his Model A Ford if they filled it up with gas when they got back.

Gasoline was 11 cents a gallon.

Johnston had several jobs at that time. "If we could find a quarter apiece, we could go to the Odeon Theatre in Shawnee and see a show for 10 cents each, and use the 15 cents left over for a hamburger and a Coke and if it was a cheap one, you could get a nickel back, but normally, we'd get a 10 cent hamburger and a nickel Coke."

That adds up to a quarter each. Where did they get the money for the 11-cent gas to fill up the Model A?

They would get drip gas, Johnston remembers. "Drip gas runs off of an oil well while it is pumping," he said. "If you dip off the top, it's gasoline and would burn in a car, but the bottom is water.

"It's waste; trash they're getting rid of."

When they were ready to start back home, the boys would get the drip gas out of the ground and put it in the car's gas tank. However, they would also get a little water which would collect in the engine and cause it to quit running if not drained off. The boys knew a process to separate the water from the gas in a Model A Ford so for them, drip gas worked just fine.

"The Model A car was a really good car," Johnston said.

When Johnston came back to Shawnee from the Army at the end of World War II, he was elected a delegate to the annual state Methodist Church conference.

"Preacher said, 'you haven't been before and you can go with me and I'll show you the rounds,' " Johnston recalled.

"We were sitting there and he said, 'that's Dr. Hamilton on the stage. He is the district superintendent.' I said, Dr. Hamilton my foot. That's Argus!"

His pastor told him to be quiet but Johnston was so excited to see his old friend, he couldn't stop talking.

"When it was over, Argus came down from the pulpit, hugged me and said, 'it's been years since I've seen you but we remember Earlsboro, don't we?'

"Preacher couldn't believe I knew him. Then Argus said, 'we used to steal drip gas to go to the show.'

"Preacher's mouth just fell open," Johnston remembers.

Another strong influence: the Christian Biblical teachings of the Masonic Lodge and the people he associated with in it as he progressed through all its chairs, became a Knight Commander Cross of Honor and Knight York Cross of Honor holder, member of the Shrine Club that operates 21 hospitals that help children in the U.S. and Canada, and Sojourners, the military wing "that also does a lot of good," he said.

One of Sojourners' projects is sending pastors to Jerusalem.

W.R. Griggs, secretary of Shawnee Masonic Lodge 107 when Johnston was worshipful master, is an additional person he remembers warmly. "Griggs helped get uniforms from the McAlester Consistory for our use in putting on patriotic programs in Shawnee and Pottawatomie County school systems," Johnston said.

Bill Ford, with whom he's met weekly since about 2005, has had a large impact on his life, the retired Army major said.

"In addition to being owner and operator of Shawnee Milling Company, Mr. Ford is also vice-chairman of the Oklahoma Veterans Memorial Park committee in Shawnee. He was the driver behind getting this moving; the mover and shaker of this program," Johnston said.

Through Ford's leadership and expertise, Johnston continued, the memorial in downtown Shawnee's Woodland Veterans Park in 2012 contained a monument centered by an American flag surrounded by flags of the five branches of U.S. military service, with 1,000 or more bricks inlaid within the monument's star-shaped base and approaches, each honoring one or more veterans of America's wars.

It stands behind a black marble archway bearing the memorial's name overhead and images of a World War I doughboy and soldier of World War II, Korean or Vietnam era engraved on its supports. At night, special lighting lining the wide walkway leading to the black marble arch and the star, appears to bring the two servicemen engravings to life.

Suspended in mid-air as though to land momentarily at the monument, is an authentic Vietnam-era Huey helicopter with a black cat design on its nose, just like the one Ford's brother, Bob Ford, Okeene, Oklahoma, flew more than 1,000 combat missions in Vietnam and received the Distinguished Flying Cross for his service.

Black benches are there and two concrete hardstands await the placement of 105 Howitzers when received. Fencing of white roping and capped metal posts like a fence in Arlington National Cemetery was installed around the memorial's perimeter.

Ford's "ability to get this done helped keep the program moving," Johnston said.

"We still lack funding for a major granite type monument listing the names of the over 6,000 Oklahomans who gave their lives in the service of their country, going back to the Spanish American War, forward," he said. A Quonset hut museum to house veterans' wartime memorabilia is planned as the final phase.

Johnston has served as an Army representative on the original seven-veteran committee since weekly meetings began about 2005.

Two more friends who have had an impact on his life, reported Johnston's extensive community service activities to Oklahoma City's KFOR-TV Channel 4 in spring 2012 and won him a $400 award – which he donated to four charitable causes in Shawnee.

Bud Mullens and Howard Fowler, both of Shawnee, were the pair who turned his name into the TV station. Longtime television personality Linda Cavanaugh made the on-air award presentation.

Johnston appeared on the television station's 10 p.m. newscast in his motorized wheelchair, which he told Cavanaugh was his Porsche.

An Oklahoma City man, a member of the Porsche Club of Oklahoma, happened to see the presentation on TV.

He drove to Shawnee's Senior Citizens Center twice to try to find Johnston, but was unsuccessful both times.

When he didn't catch Johnston on the second attempt, he left two Porsche stickers for Johnston to attach to his wheelchair.

Thixe Totty, Shawnee RSVP director at the center, reported, "the two times he has been here, he has been all over Shawnee looking for Cecil Johnston."

The wheelchair now bears the Porsche name (or at least a decal to that effect).

Johnston had grateful feelings for all involved, especially for Fowler and Mullens who started it all…and for other lasting guidance the two men had given him in recent months.

"As I go back and think about it, I just can't believe some of the things I've seen," Johnston said.

"I've seen people killed in action, but to me, the abuse of kids is one of the worst things. To see kids have to suffer and not receive due consideration for their life and their right to exist.

"It was always heart breaking."

Johnston remembers children hungry, reaching down into "that slop" in garbage cans on the backs of Army trucks, "and grabbing anything they could get, to eat."

Johnston's first thought was of the rations he and the other servicemen had. "I wanted to get an interpreter and tell them, 'here, I'll give you some food but don't eat that slop.' "

Another memory that sticks with him even after 65 years or more was the day he was informed a couple wanted to see him- and advised "you won't believe what they want."

"A family in North Africa wanted to sell a child for $10,000 if we'd run over it," Johnston said.

Army caravans had to travel at night with only a thin sliver of headlights on, in an attempt to avoid enemy detection. A truck had accidentally struck and killed one of the couple's children. The U.S. government had paid them $10,000 in damages.

"They could have another child but not a chance at another $10,000," Johnston said.

He conveyed his deep sympathy on the death of the first child but firmly said "no way" to their new request.

"But I saw the effects of the Marshall Plan in the occupation – how it brought those countries out from being destitute after the war to where their people would walk off jobs Americans were offering them because they could get better jobs that their own governments were offering.

"I saw the impact of what the Marshall Plan did to help them recover from the war."

So World War II "was bad, bad, but it wasn't all bad because we kept our country from being eaten up. Everybody here would be speaking Deutsch or Russian if it wasn't for the sacrifices of about 2 million Americans," Johnston said.

"I come back to one thing: I made a covenant with the Lord in

World War II because I needed help to beat the pressures of the time and place I was in.

"The Lord kept His part and I'm trying my best to do everything I promised the Lord. I'm trying to help all His children here to the best of my ability.

"The Lord has been really good to me over the years. I've found some wonderful people in this world.

"I've got reasonably good health and my memory; had two good wives and five kids; was able to bring all of them and their kids to Europe, paid their way and gave them a tour of someplace in Europe-Switzerland, Netherlands, France, Nuremberg, Bavaria or elsewhere-trying to help."

Johnston had a lot of good friends "over there. My German neighbor from whom we rented thought I walked on water because I paid our rent on time."

He remembers a one way street that came to a bend on a hillside. He installed a mirror, so drivers could see what was around the corner. "The people thought it was really great. They called me 'mayor' after that.

"They would put me to work when they had a strassenfest (street fair). Louise and I would be the ticket-takers. I did things like that trying to be helpful to our community.

"I was nice to people. Louise and I would bake bread and deliver it to all the neighbors."

Johnston had his own recipe for handling any post traumatic depression he might have brought home from World War II.

"Rather than go to the doctor and take pills, I acquired some land at Shawnee Twin Lakes and would revert back to my childhood. I hoed and spaded it up and planted a garden. Then I would sit back and listen to the birds and the wild animals. "When the whippoorwills started singing, I knew it was time to go home.

"I no longer have it, but it served its purpose for me."

That agricultural interlude in his life reminded Johnston of one of his father's favorite sayings: "When the wind is blowing from the east, it's neither fit for man nor beast. When the wind is from the north, the wise man goeth not forth. When the wind is from the south, it blows the bait into the fish's mouth and when the wind is from the west, fishing is at it very best!"

And he passes along that the expression, "bawling like a dying calf in a hail storm" originated from calves dying during birth in heavy rainstorms if humans didn't save them.

Johnston's Grandpa Isaac Johnston and his beloved Grandpa John Smith were poles apart. Grandpa Smith grew corn and turned it into liquid gold for himself, his family, friends and neighbors. He bought the first automobile in Atoka County and had a letter from Washington advising that if anyone in the county needed anything, see Whiskey John Smith, who was also the county commissioner.

"The Johnston family was very religious, hell fire and damnation lay preachers and one of the buildings some of them helped build in southeast Missouri is still named Johnston Chapel," Cecil Johnston said. Grandpa Johnston, of Morris, and later Nowata, Oklahoma, was one of the clan.

"We used to have Johnston family reunions every year. Grandpa Johnston had 125 living descendants and most would be there. The reunions were held at different places, normally at someone's farm; but they were not corn liquor farmers," he said, emphasizing the 'not.'

One of Johnston's great-great-grandparents was Joseph E. Johnston, a general in the Civil War.

He has a great-grandfather on his mother, Idaho Montana Johnston's side, who was an Arkansas judge called a "hanging judge."

And a great-great-great grandmother named Katherine House, was a Cherokee Indian from North Carolina. Her daughter was married in 1804, records state, so Johnston figures Katherine House might have been born around Revolutionary War times.

He's learned lots along the way...

"I've tried to use a little common horse sense.

"Do it right the first time. Think about what you need to do and put it in the right sequence so you won't have to do it all over again.

"For example, if you need to turn the light off, do it the first time. Don't forget and have to go back again and do it. You're wasting time. This could make you late to work."

"Don't buy things before you can afford them. Don't buy a washer if you can't afford it. Wash clothes on a washboard and save up for it.

"If you don't know how to manage your time and your money, you're not going to have either one very long.

"Don't give up just because you stumble and fall. Don't give up; learn from your mistakes. And don't blame others for your mistakes.

"Don't think you have to gripe about everything that's dealt you. If you're dealt a bad hand, just play the game and go on. Life is too short to sit around and complain about something.

"I've met some really nice people over all my travels. A whole lot more nice people than I found bad. And the bad ones I found might have been that way because maybe I didn't do something right."

Johnston recalled a story he used to tell his Boy Scouts.

"These people were moving into a new town. They found this man sitting in the shade of a tree. They asked him what the people were like in this neighborhood.

"What were they like where you're moving from?" the man asked. "They were fantastic," the people replied. "Everybody was friendly. Everybody helped each other. That's one reason why we hate to move, because our neighbors were so good."

The man's remark was, "you'll find the people are exactly the same right here."

Johnston said he told his Scouts the other side of the story. "When they said their neighbors were terrible, the man said, 'that's what you'll find here.'

"People are going to reflect how you act," Johnston said he told the Scouts.

"As the Bible says, do unto others as you would have them do unto you."

He hopes folks remember the Lord helps those who help themselves.

But he also knows, "you can't force things on people. Offer them the benefit of your experience. If they don't want it? So we've still got a free country and that's what we fought the war for, to have a free country.

"I think the world is going to go on in spite of whatever we do but I am concerned about the economy because if we go through another depression, I'm not sure the people understand how to exist when you don't have anything. They are so used to being pampered and having money and having all their wants and desires met.

"When they get down to needing the necessities, how are they going to handle it?

"If you don't have $2,000 coming in every month and you only have 25 cents, how can they cope?

"We had a cow for milk, pigs for meat in the wintertime, a garden from which you canned everything, all your vegetables, and fruit trees.

"But today, would people know what to do if they didn't have a big paycheck coming in? They don't know how to live off the land. I'm not sure we've passed this along to the younger generation if we run into another depression like the 1930s.

"But I have faith somebody would come along and lead. The Lord would find somebody." Johnston said.

Remembering his Grandpa Smith telling him as a boy, to hold up his end of a cross-cut saw, not drag it, Johnston said he has "tried to live a good life and tried to contribute."